THE SPECTRUM HAIKU

John Mickus

First Published in the United States of America
First Edition.

ISBN: 978-0-6151-7725-0

Copyright © 2007, John Mickus, registered author & ISBN owner. All Rights Reserved. On-Demand publication and distribution provided by Lulu, Inc. No portion of this book may be reproduced either in print or electronic format without the expressed written consent of the author.

All Graphics and Photographs © 2007 John Mickus

6
16
26
36
46
56
66
76
86
96
106
116

Contents

1
Black begs for contrast.
And the vivid will answer—
and shock the senses!

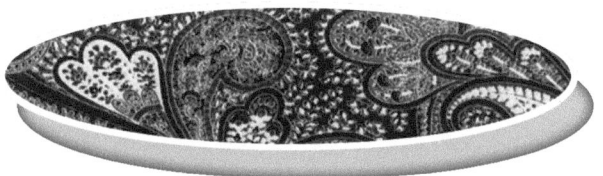

2
Jeff screamed at her hair
Avalanching velvet sheets
Massaging them both

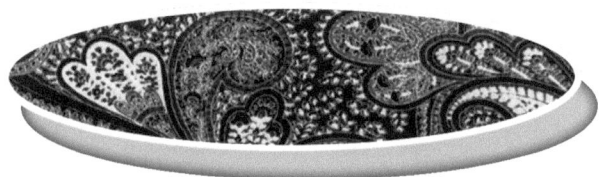

3

Deep down, inside an album,
One slow summer brightens the memory.

When the sun shined in
Through fingerprinted glass.

And with relaxing lids, you saw
The blinds slide close
And cover you with shade.

They close tighter now.
Serene it is: to remember darkness

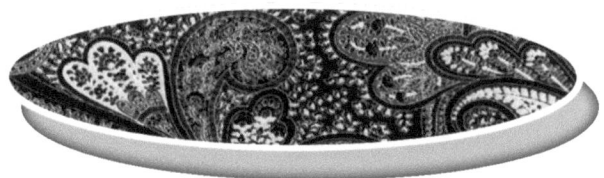

4
With a heavy heart,
The evenings became many—
But without regret.

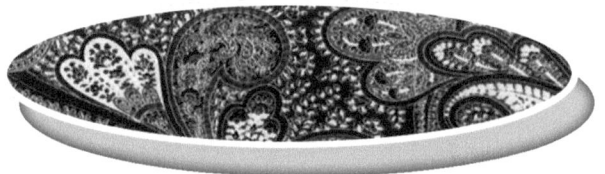

5
Hatred increases
Like a derailing train
Across black, burned grass
On a chalky, dark plain

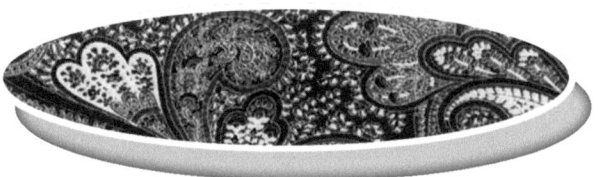

6
Understated flair
In crafted fireplaces
can showcase marble

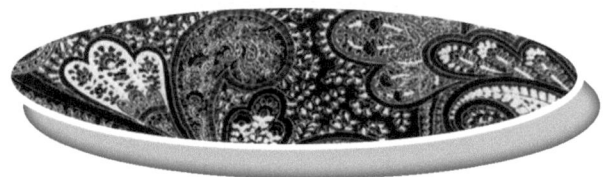

7
Earthly black business
Whipcracked its way into us;
Escape the Godless!

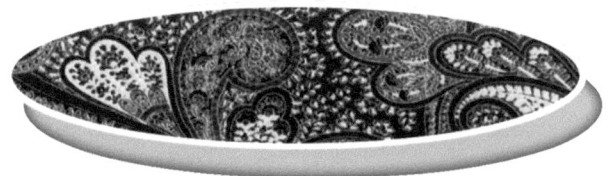

8
Leap to me with trust
Let's take our shot at wonder
And defy all else

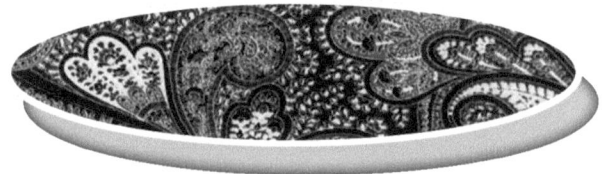

9
Sisters to the end
Dodging rumors all the way
And ignoring hurt

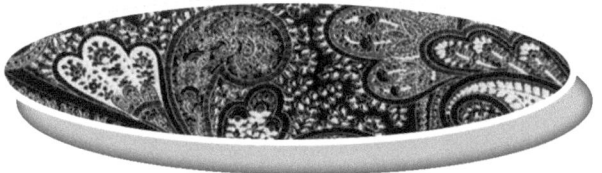

10
One flower pedal
Survives from spring. So faded…
Yet the pink still Moves.

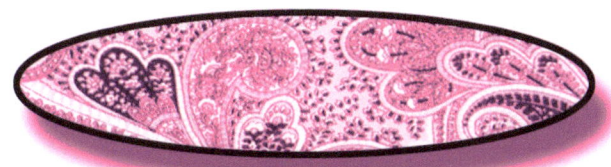

11
The fairest lip's edge
is faded from its brighter
cousins of sharp reds

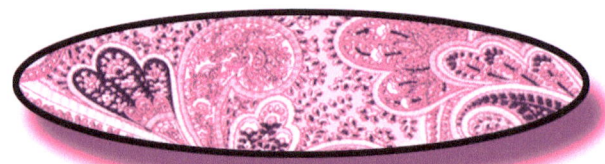

12
Some graceful pink cloaks
hide jeweled angels dancing
in a frozen crowd

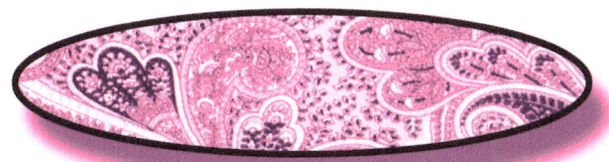

13
Seven polished pearls
Kissed with the gentlest blush
Given at dessert

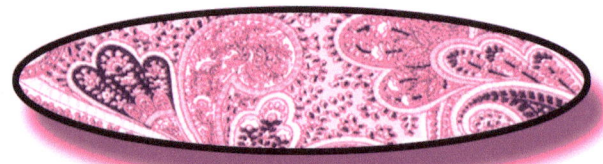

14
Fired between blurs
The most feminine colors
alive by fuchsia

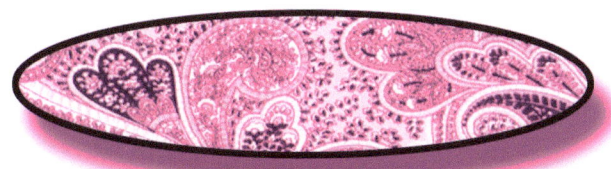

15
A complex soft shield
Protects our silent heartbeat.
Fragile life lives quick

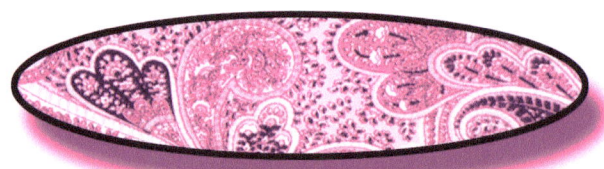

16
She studied his face.
In a short dress, she stood up—
Accepting the ring

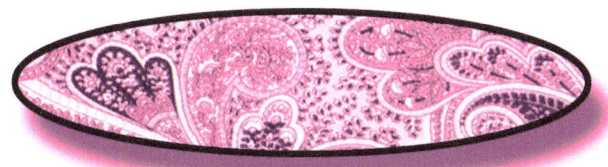

17
With our ears ringing,
We stumbled down the sidewalk
With our cheeks touching

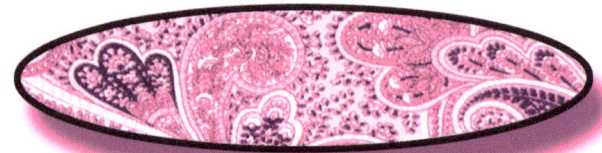

25

gray

18
Today, size and time
Move at crooked pace
The smiling man kills
With no wrinkling face

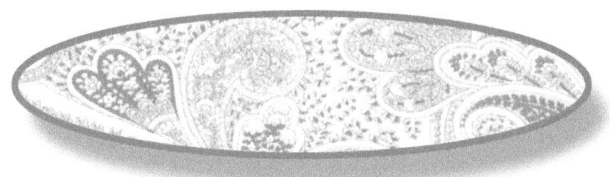

19
A plastic office
on an unused boulevard
can still be your goal

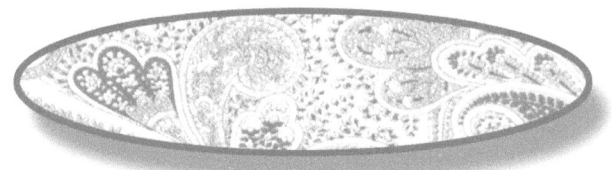

20
One fashionable jogger
With one bright stripe
Always in ultimate gray
At morning light

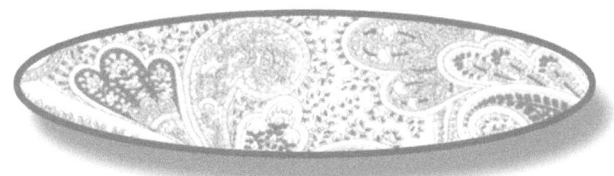

21
Paper mountains fade,
A dull façade clings tightly
to greed (so slightly)

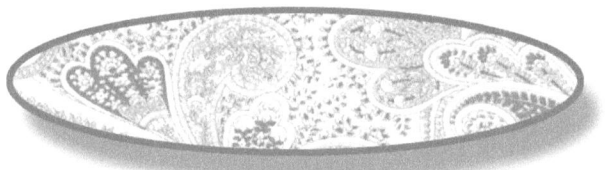

22
The old explorer
Missed his stubborn whiskers but
Not as much as salt

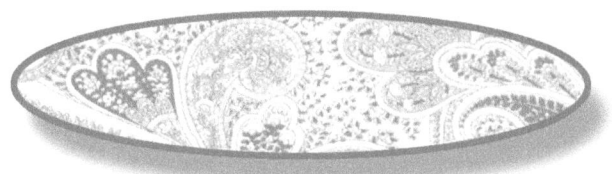

23
He who wonders
How the prickly Future
Could be touched

He who will not know
How small flowers thrived
Falling down the dusty spiral
Of dirty apathy
And hate

Playing where the Good people wouldn't
Is what saves the Wrong in this world.

Durable, like a stone umbrella,
The little things are what might stay…
Around us, and Above us
To pull a day's colors
Away from gray

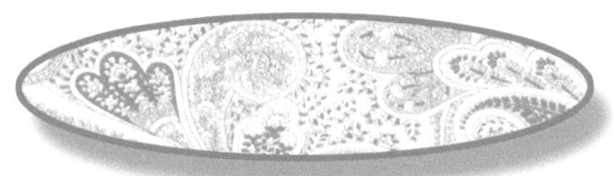

24
Smart minds on the edge
Bring the full world to its knees
With battles between

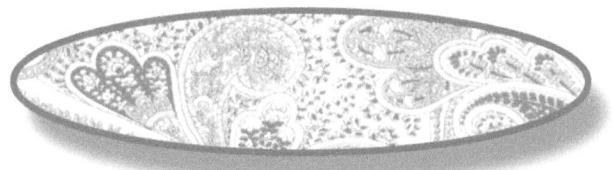

25
You've impressed no one—
You have read too many books.
I've defined success

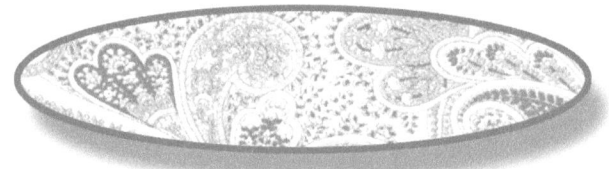

green

26
The wind blows all the way through the trees.
The palms reflect too, adding warmth to the breeze.

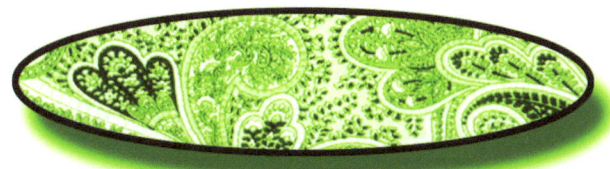

27
Tickling the cliff's edge,
Very small bushes bloom.
Pouring their green
into the ocean air.

28
Rustling fresh mint,
Around a plantation skirt
Makes easy waves of charm.

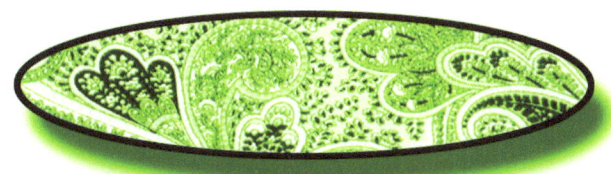

29
Galactic cities
Of books and our future near
With new night skylines

30
New, swift nutrition
Will take the best of the bland
Along with the sweet

31
So far from home now...
Our adventure pauses us
in hot jungle rain

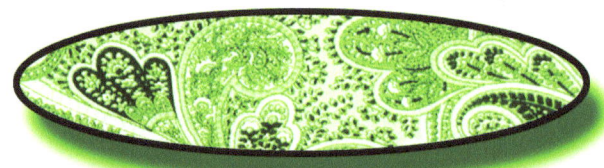

32
Clean-cut champions
In ironed uniforms wait
For commands to act

33
We knew we were fools
When we saw the water change.
...should have brought a knife.

whïte

34
All who live can see
Even the faintest light.
But usually—or only—when it's dark.

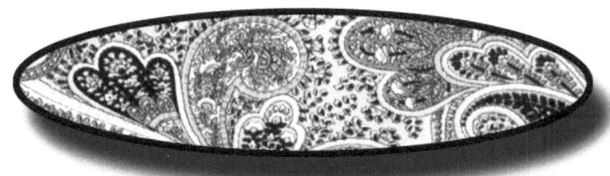

35
Far beyond the patio
Lay an impossible array
Of lights
Urban and quiet…
These are the white-hot stars that keep the night alive
When one sits cold,
Comfortably on the patio

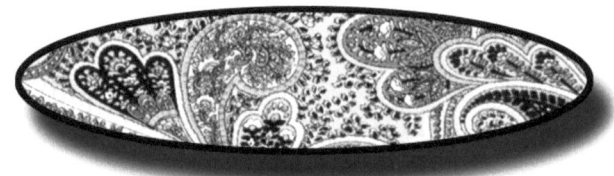

36
Light saunters into
windows overhead. Traces
fall abundantly.

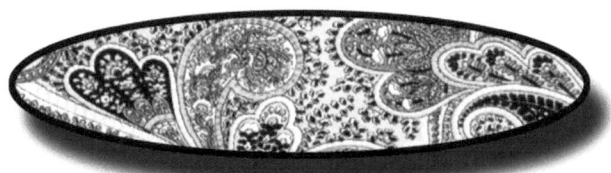

37
It was dark, now light
Now it's all mixed together
From one ray of light

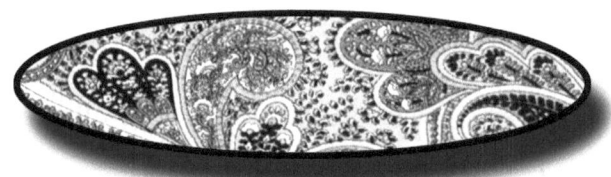

38
With Godly device,
I converse in brevity—
One forgotten art!

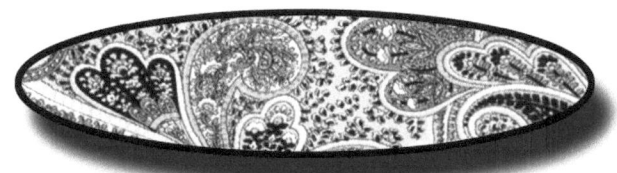

39
Maybe just one night
with fancy white tablecloth
Might have helped save us.

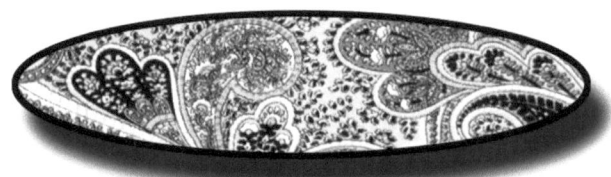

40
Optical assault
Calls for the whitest white dress
With explosive dots

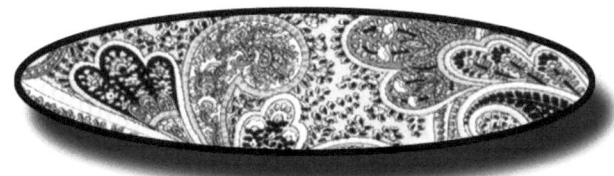

41
A small, pretty girl
Makes herself stand far apart
With only her smile

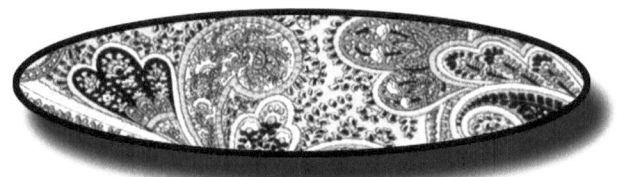

42
The science of a sunset
Lost…
In its blistering beauty
Lost in a storm of reds

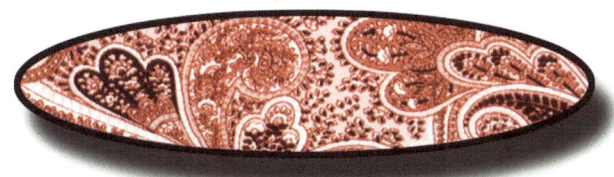

43
Cherry red berries
Resting on a block of ice
So cold and supple

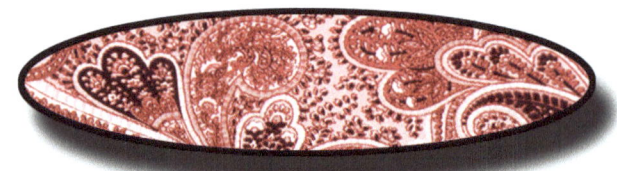

44
When I felt alone,
It was a permanent scar—
Love taketh away.

45
Simplicity without pretense,
design becomes art with order.
A red dot in a sky of veneered boast,
A lack of complication
can be the line between the most.

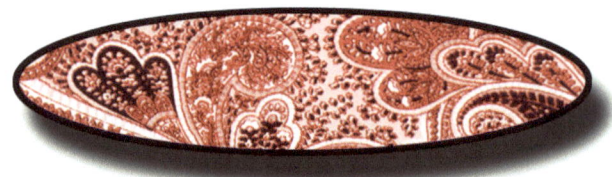

46
Somewhere in cities,
There is always one structure—
Brick and forgotten

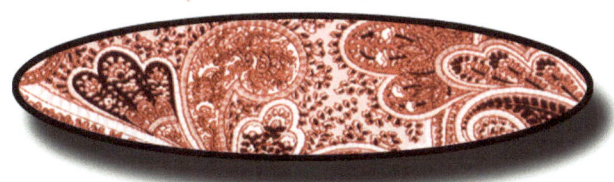

47
As a touchstone of love
she worries about his flight
With a crystal glass of wine
on a San Diego night

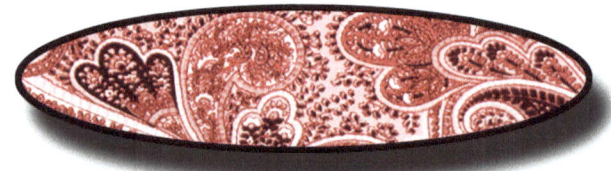

48
Out of the traffic
Comes dinner off the clean stove
(With a quiet show)

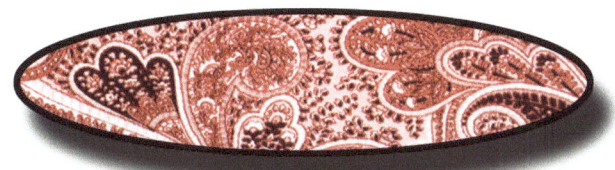

49
Even in a Porsche,
Where quality is complete—
Detail prevails

50
A spicy girlfriend
Spawns jealousy and envy
In a classy way

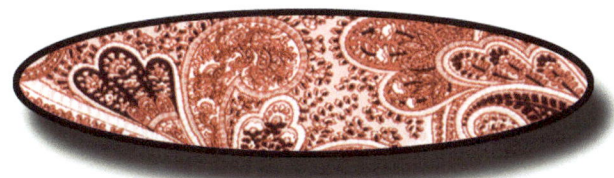

51
The sun-cracked sandals hide under the wood bench
(Where the good beach towel is draped.)
The blurry summertime makes everything squint,
While the Friday pavement is baked.

52
With toasted sand under my feet, I run and fear my own self.
Glistening and panting
But staying aware
Terrible pain here
And death over there

53
Like in the old days,
The railroad track is alone—
And always in the right place.

54
The dead leaves will give
Just a little bit of crunch—
Before dirt hardens your foot.

55
Bottled warm water
Rests… shelved in the desert—
Cool at store closing

56
A guitar in Greece
Rubbed with light clay in places
In the smallest town

57
Behind chintzy doors
Lives a lonely debonair
With candlelit scotch

58
Curfewless kitten
sneaks left, and out of the mud—
away from noises

59
Violin thunder
With no echo but with force
Carries Tiffany

60
Neither of us knew much
About that old, flat valley.
But corn there was crisp.

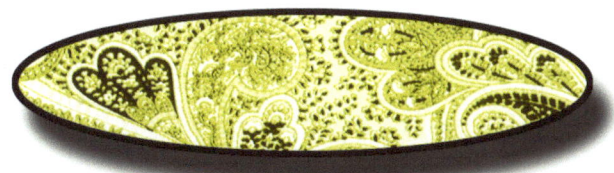

61
Butter on my toast:
Apoplectically rich,
Makes this meal perfect.

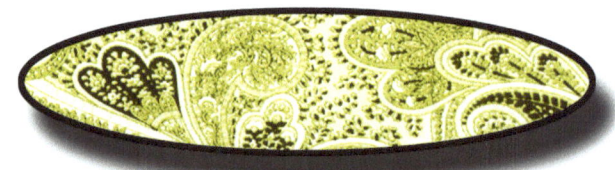

62
Correct a vandal:
Criticize his yellow streaks,
But ponder his cause.

63
French vanilla wax
Melted and solid in parts
Steadies the wick's flame

64
Beware the sharp wit:
It can cut or it can heal
"New Philanthropy"

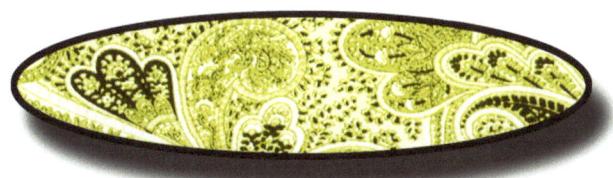

65
A pale sky watches
The bright ball fly and almost
Destroy the racquet

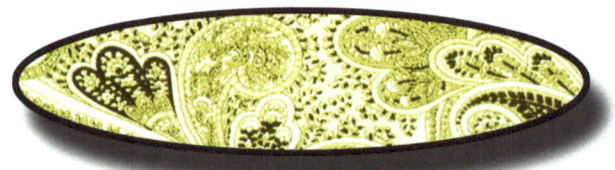

66
Tall, thin, golden grass
Brushed against the lion's paw
And its eyes focused

67
I knew she wanted
When she wore the special coat.
But it was worth it.

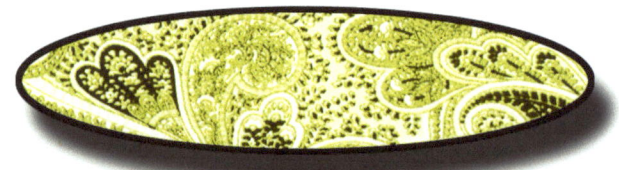

85

68
Soft, hard pulp of orange...
Zesty, and bright with flavor!
Goes best with breakfast.

69
Tangerine candy
molten on my dashboard
the lights of my car
bring me to the beach,
Lighting up dusk.

70
A night soaked with dance
can greet a modest aubade…
With the sun's first tear.

71
Inside a holiday,
A stillness can be noticed.
Warm with the weather
from the separation of life
outside of the racing things—
farthest from paradise and strife.

72
Different kinds of smoke
Rising from a family's place...
(Unbuilt and inflamed)

73
Vibrant, silky suits
Are refrigerated heat
In the bar tonight

74
Somewhere in Sweden
My brother told me of fields
Covered with color

75
Our cameras swayed
Below some amber streetlights
and we saw our breath

76
A warm winter day
A long pier is deserted...
With no sign of why.

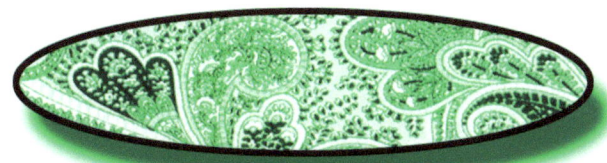

77
That jewelry I gave you
had the color I've never seen.
I wanted you to own it...
Before its hue was part of the sea.

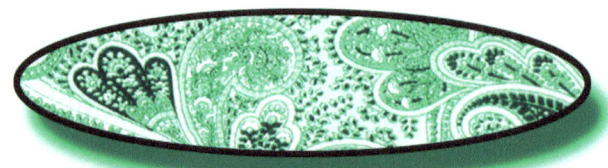

78
A piercing eye's glance
Holds pieces of all the best
Imagination.

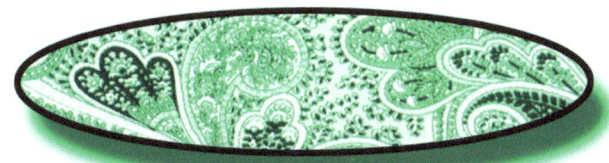

79
Bartending talent:
What proportions shall you pick?
From this year, to the next…

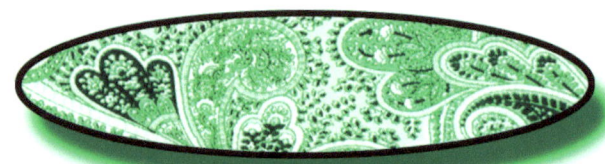

80
Crime is getting
International and worse—
Organized with yachts

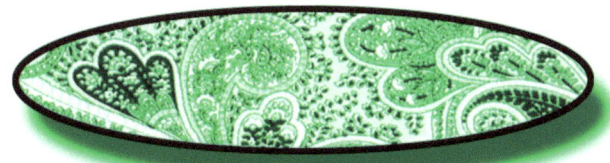

81
With great jobs, they sat...
Embracing in luxury,
Near sparkled fountains

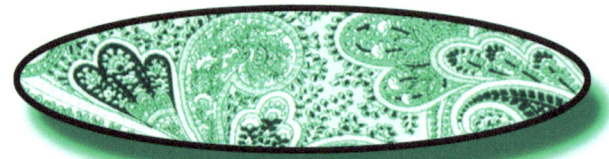

82
Malibu under
Her painted fingernails
Gave her a beach smell

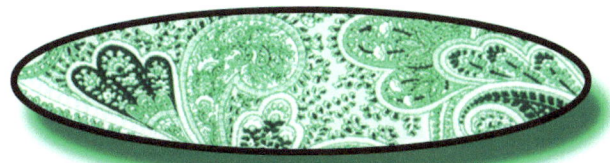

83
Across a table—
An apology is real.
Alone. Together. Tonight.

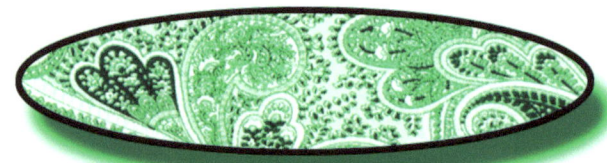

84
Is blue the same, in
Monaco or anywhere?
From seeing, you'll know.

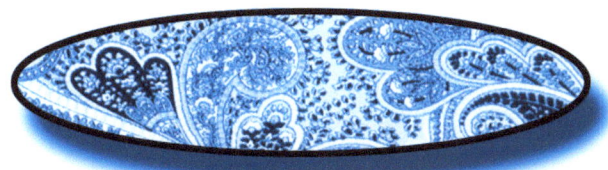

85
Walking out into the summer,
The door closes behind me.

The door closes silently
And I walk wildly
Looking at the sky and smiling

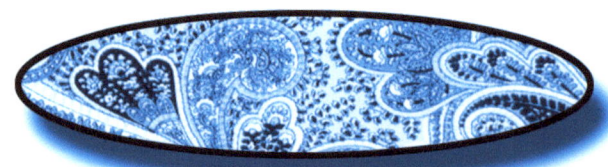

86
Daily barrage of daylight,
Her heart needs heat from you!
Thriving, amidst the ices,
Her eyes burn cold but true.

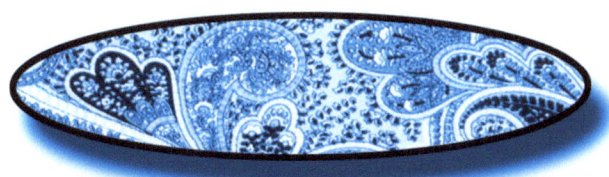

87
Modern sapphire skies
smudge ancient exotic trees
barely sliding dark

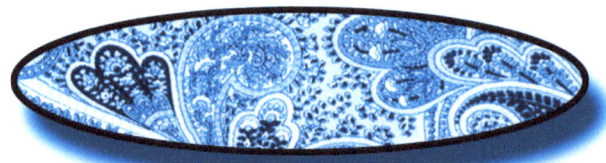

88
The finest leather
Rich with seedless blueberry
Fitted and too soft

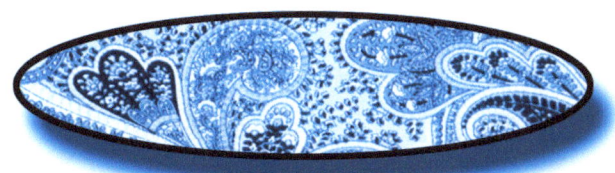

89
Father's cloudy boat
Made the traveling seem longer.
...creaking...loud tonight

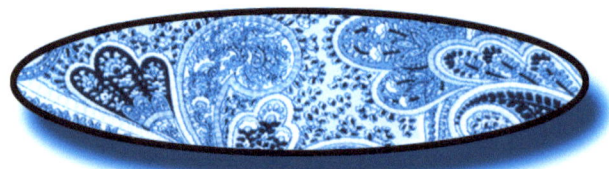

90
Jagged emotion
Speeds him to a hospital
To bring a flower

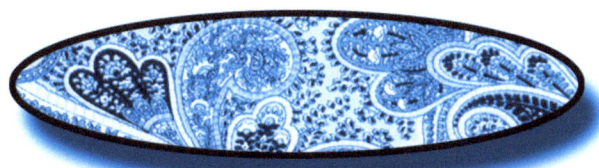

91
Peering through the stare
A genuine moment there,
Under satin sheets

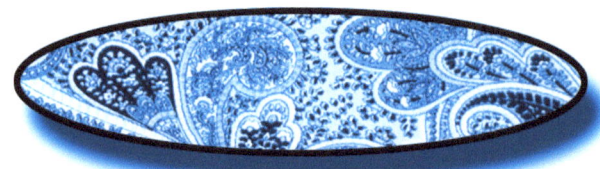

92
The purple house
On the busy street
Was painted yesterday
In a summer's heat

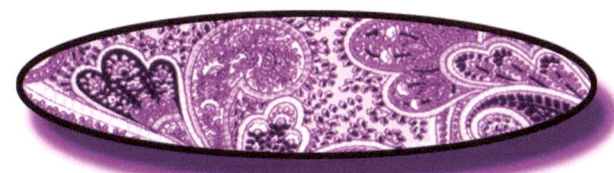

93
In the twilight breeze,
A silent, purple backyard
Seems timeless to me

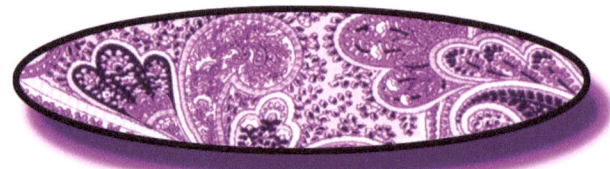

94
Strange, uncommon trees
disperse rainbows to the ground—
Darkened and untouched.

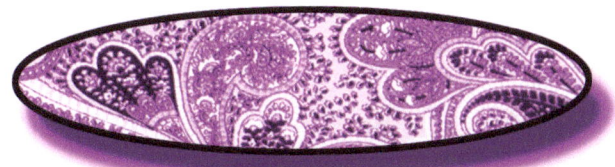

95
How bold of a flag—
Would wine coloring assist?
To earn One salute?

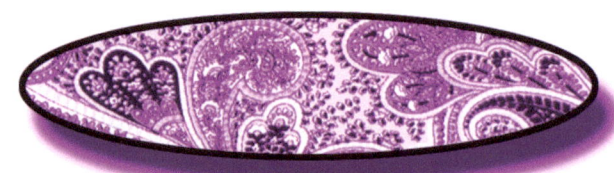

96
Dark nights of neon
Hide a room with purple shine
behind solemn glow

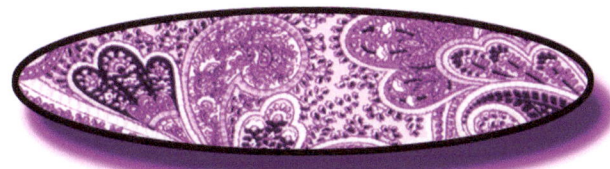

97
Piano and snare
Bring us back and slow down time...
Show us destiny.

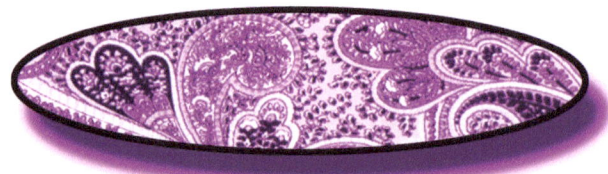

98
Precious black diamonds
Throw sinister tricks of glare
Into high fashion

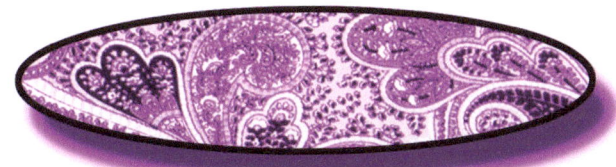

99
Quietly close to me
just wearing expensive lipstick,
she told me about our night.

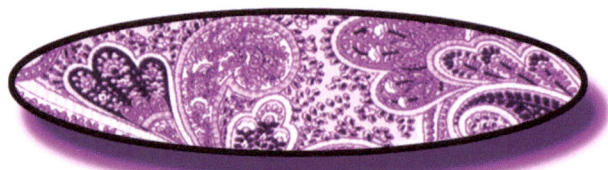

www.ingramcontent.com/pod-product-compliance
Lightning Source LLC
Chambersburg PA
CBHW041403020526
44115CB00036B/9